CONTENTS

In this book, you will learn about

concert bands

what they are

where you can see them

and much more!

Flutes toot.
Cymbals crash.

CONCERT BANDS

Ruth Daly

BANDS    

www.av2books.com

Go to www.av2books.com, and enter this book's unique code.

BOOK CODE

AVM42423

AV² by Weigl brings you media enhanced books that support active learning.

AV² provides enriched content that supplements and complements this book. Weigl's AV² books strive to create inspired learning and engage young minds in a total learning experience.

Your AV² Media Enhanced books come alive with...

Audio
Listen to sections of the book read aloud.

Video
Watch informative video clips.

Embedded Weblinks
Gain additional information for research.

Try This!
Complete activities and hands-on experiments.

Key Words
Study vocabulary, and complete a matching word activity.

Quizzes
Test your knowledge.

Slide Show
View images and captions, and prepare a presentation.

... and much, much more!

Published by AV² by Weigl
350 5th Avenue, 59th Floor New York, NY 10118
Website: www.av2books.com

Library of Congress Control Number: 2019938591

ISBN 978-1-7911-1118-2 (hardcover)
ISBN 978-1-7911-1119-9 (softcover)
ISBN 978-1-7911-1120-5 (multi-user eBook)
ISBN 978-1-7911-1121-2 (singler-user eBook)

Printed in Guangzhou, China
1 2 3 4 5 6 7 8 9 0 23 22 21 20 19

062019
311018

Project Coordinator: Heather Kissock Designer: Terry Paulhus

Weigl acknowledges Getty Images, Alamy, Shutterstock, and Wikimedia as the primary image suppliers for this title. Page 1 and 17: Senior Airman Steele C. G. Britton, U.S. Air Force.

The conductor leads the band. Concert bands are entertaining.

Concert bands lift people's spirits. People come to hear the upbeat music.

ELMIRA
CORNET
BAND
ECB
8

Concert bands became popular in the United States during the Civil War. Their songs helped soldiers feel brave.

The U.S. Army Concert Band was formed in 1922. It played for soldiers who were far away from home.

Today, the **U.S. Army Concert Band** performs more than **100 concerts** every year.

Concert bands play music that many people know. They also perform songs from long ago.

Concert bands use many different instruments. Some people play trumpets. Others play French horns. Drums and cymbals are also used.

There are between **40 and 80 people** in a concert band.

The conductor keeps the band on beat. He or she waves a short stick called a baton.

A concert band usually performs in a concert hall. Band members often wear black and white clothes.

A concert lasts for about **two hours**. There is sometimes a break halfway through.

Carnegie Hall is a popular concert hall in New York City. More than 3,600 people can sit inside for concerts.

See what you have learned about concert bands.

Which of these pictures is not a concert band?

KEY WORDS

Research has shown that as much as 65 percent of all written material published in English is made up of 300 words. These 300 words cannot be taught using pictures or learned by sounding them out. They must be recognized by sight. This book contains 61 common sight words to help young readers improve their reading fluency and comprehension. This book also teaches young readers several important content words, such as proper nouns. These words are paired with pictures to aid in learning and improve understanding.

Page	Sight Words First Appearance
5	are, the
7	come, hear, people, to
9	in, songs, states, their
10	away, every, far, for, from, home, it, more, than, was, were, who, year
13	also, know, long, many, play, that, they
14	a, and, between, different, others, some, there, use
17	he, keeps, on, or, she
18	about, is, lasts, often, sometimes, through, two, white
20	can
22	have, not, of, pictures, see, these, what, which, you

Page	Content Words First Appearance
4	cymbals, flutes
5	concert bands, conductor
7	music, spirits
9	Civil War, soldiers, United States
10	U.S. Army Concert Band
14	drums, French horns, instruments, trumpets
17	baton, beat, stick
18	break, clothes, concert hall, hours
20	Carnegie Hall, New York City

Check out www.av2books.com for activities, videos, audio clips, and more!

1. Go to www.av2books.com.
2. Enter book code. **AVM42423**
3. Fuel your imagination online!

www.av2books.com